Capybaras

Victoria Blakemore

For Madi and Brady, can you "beleaf" I finally finished it?

Thank for you always sharing your awesome ideas! 🍃

Copyright info/picture credits

Table of Contents

What Are Capybaras?

Capybaras are the largest kind of rodent. They are related to other rodents such as guinea pigs and chinchillas.

Capybaras are semi-aquatic mammals. This means that they spend a lot of their time in the water.

They are often called "water pigs" because they spend so much time in the water.

Size

Adult capybaras are often between three and four feet long. They are about one and a half feet tall at the shoulder.

When fully grown, capybaras **vary** in weight. They can weigh between 60 and 170 pounds.

Male capybaras are usually larger than female capybaras.

Physical Characteristics

Capybaras are covered in an oily, water-resistant fur. It helps them when they are in the water.

They have strong teeth and jaws. This allows them to grasp and break down tough plants. They can also bite to defend themselves.

Capybaras are able to keep their eyes, ears, and nostrils out of the water while the rest of their body is hidden.

Habitat

Capybaras are found in several habitats. Marshes, grasslands, and lowland forests are their preferred habitats.

They need habitats where it is very wet as much of their diet comes from water plants.

Range

Capybaras are found in Central and South America.

They are often seen in countries like Brazil, Venezuela, Panama, Colombia, and Peru.

‖

Diet

Capybara are **herbivores**, which means that they eat only plants.

Their diet is mainly made up of grasses. During the dry season, they also eat reeds, grains, melons, and squash.

Adult capybaras can eat up to eight pounds of grass each day.

Capybara have also been known to eat their own **waste**. It contains bacteria that helps their stomach break down all of the grasses that they eat.

Capybaras have strong teeth. Their teeth also help them to break down all of the tough plants they eat.

Like other rodents, capybaras

have front teeth that never stop

growing.

Communication

Capybaras use mainly sound and scent to communicate. They are very vocal and are often heard before they are seen.

Capybaras use sounds like barks to warn of danger. They also make a clicking sound when they are content.

Capybaras each have a special scent. They use it to mark their **territory** and identify other capybaras.

Movement

Capybaras have short, stocky bodies. Their size helps them to move quickly on land and in the water.

They have been known to run up to twenty-two miles per hour on land. They are also able to turn quickly.

Capybaras are great swimmers.

Their webbed feet help them to

swim.

Capybara Pups

Capybaras have one **litter** of up to eight babies each year. Their babies, or pups, are able to stand and walk shortly after they are born.

Capybaras work together to take care of pups. They help to feed and protect the pups.

Young capybaras are able to **graze** within about a week of being born.

Capybara Life

Capybaras are very **social** animals. They prefer to be in a group with other capybaras. They are often seen in groups of between ten and thirty.

Capybaras are **territorial**. They have an area that they claim as their own and they will chase other capybaras away.

Capybaras work together to

take care of pups, find food,

and defend against predators.

Staying Cool

It can be hot where capybaras live. They have special ways to stay cool.

Capybaras are often seen **wallowing** in the mud. The cool mud keeps them from **overheating**. It also keeps their skin from getting too dry.

Capybaras often rest in the middle of the day when it is the hottest.

Population

Capybaras are currently listed as **least concern**. Their populations are **stable** in the wild.

It is not known exactly how many are in the wild. They are found in many places and it can be difficult for researchers to count all of them.

In the wild, capybaras often live between six and ten years. They may live up to twelve in **captivity**.

Capybaras are very important

to their ecosystem. Many

different birds eat the insects

that capybaras stir up when

they are **grazing**.

They are also hunted for their

meat and leather by people in

South America.

Capybaras are also prey for larger animals such as jaguars, caimans, and harpy eagles.

Helping Capybaras

Capybaras are not currently in danger of becoming **extinct**, but there are still ways that they can be helped.

In many places, it is **illegal** to hunt wild capybaras. These laws help to protect capybaras from being **overhunted**.

In many places, rainforest is being cleared for logging and building. Many groups are trying to protect the rainforest to help animals such as capybaras.

Other groups focus on research and education. They want to learn as much about capybaras as they can so they can keep helping them.

Glossary

Captivity: animals that are kept by humans, not in the wild

Extinct: when there are no more of an animal left in the wild

Graze: to eat grass

Herbivore: an animal that eats only plants

Illegal: against the law

Least concern: when an animal's population is stable and they are not in danger of becoming extinct

Litter: a group of animals born at the same time

Overheat: to get too hot

Overhunted: when too many animals are hunted, causing the population to decline

Social: living in groups

Stable: unchanging

Territorial: when an animal is protective of its territory

Territory: an area of land that an animal claims as its own

Wallow: to roll around in mud or water

Waste: material given off by the body after food is digested

Vary: differ

About the Author

Victoria Blakemore is a first grade

teacher in Southwest Florida with a

passion for reading.

You can visit her at

www.elementaryexplorers.com

Also in This Series

Elementary Explorers

y Wolves	Sloths	Flamingos	Camels	Koalas	Honey Bees	Pandas
ngolins	White-Tailed Deer	Orcas	Giraffes	Corn	Meerkats	Echidnas
lruses	Raccoons	Bald Eagles	Apples	Arctic Foxes	Red Pandas	Cassowaries
igers	Ladybugs	Moose	Beluga Whales	Leopards	Elephants	Jellyfish
urongs	Lions	Dolphins	Reindeer	Hammerhead Sharks	Hippos	Pumpkins
afowl	Chameleons	Florida Panthers	Aye-Ayes	Black Bears	Cheetahs	Manatees
erbread	Polar Bears	Hot Chocolate	Orangutans	Coyotes	Marshmallows	Strawberries

Victoria Blakemore

Also in This Series

Aardvarks	Mako Sharks	Alligators	Frogs	Hedgehogs	Brown Bears	Bongo
Sea Turtles	Quokkas	Muskrats	Zebras	Red Foxes	Ring-Tailed Lemurs	Platypu
Anteaters	Kangaroos	Rhinos	Jaguars	Wombats	Capybaras	Goril
Cats	Skunks	Butterflies	Dingoes	Snow Leopards	African Wild Dogs	Pengu
Whale Sharks	Wolverines	Warthogs	Caracals	Badgers	Seals	Hummin
Pikas	Humpback Whales	Pumas	Lemonade	Llamas	Tulips	Ostric
Sunflowers	Fennec Foxes	Sea Lions	Squirrels	Roses	Porcupines	Ice Cr

Victoria Blakemore

www.ingramcontent.com/pod-product-compliance
Lightning Source LLC
Chambersburg PA
CBHW051251020426
42333CB00025B/3152